The Holly Wreath Man

To Joanne
Love
Amelia
12/25/2005

The Holly Wreath Man

by CHRISTOPHER SCANLAN
and KATHARINE FAIR

**Andrews McMeel
Publishing**

Kansas City

THE HOLLY WREATH MAN

05 06 07 08 09 WKT 10987654321

ISBN-13: 978-0-7407-5491-3
ISBN-10: 0-7407-5491-2
Library of Congress Control Number: 2005921392

Book design by Diane Marsh

FOR PETIE and LOUISE,
our MOTHERS;

and

CAITLIN, LIANNA, and MICHAELA,
our DAUGHTERS

Contents

CONTENTS

The Holly Wreath Man

CHAPTER 1

Missing

Jeff Henderson's life was full, too full. And at the moment, it was full of trouble. Stacks of computer printouts covered every inch of his desk. It would take another two days of number crunching to finish the marketing report.

It was due tomorrow morning. He put up his RABID DOG: DO NOT ENTER sign, shut the office door, and hunkered down in front of the computer.

When the door opened a crack, and a hand waving a white hankie reached in, he had to smile.

"What is it, Cheryl?"

"Sorry." His assistant winced. "It's your wife. She said it's an emergency."

Jeff felt his heart race. Maybe Rachel wanted him back? He took a deep breath and picked up the phone. Careful, he told himself.

"Hey," he said. "What's up?"

"The kids aren't with you, are they?"

There was panic in Rachel's voice.

"What?" he said. "Of course not."

"Well, they didn't come home from school. The bus drove by without even stopping. I figured they missed it again; you know how Katie dawdles. But when they didn't call . . ." She caught her breath.

"Now wait a sec. What about band practice?"

"That's Monday, Jeff."

He clenched the receiver. Forgetting the kids' schedules had been one of Rachel's major complaints to their marriage counselor. "Gosh," he backpedaled. "Is it Tuesday already?"

"I dropped them at the car rider's circle this morning, but the office has them marked absent. Jeff, I'm scared."

Jeff's gaze caught the spreadsheet on his monitor. He knew what she wanted from him, but an invisible chain bound him to his desk. "Have you called their friends?"

"Of course. No one has seen them. I've called the police."

"What?"

"You have to come home, Jeff. Now."

He saved the computer file and grabbed his coat.

"I'll be back," he told Cheryl. "Can you print out what's on my screen?"

"Is everything okay?"

"Sure."

"Do you want me to ask Susan to finish the report?" Susan was the newest member of the marketing research team, a bright, young MBA eager to pitch in, and, Jeff feared, claim his turf.

"No, no. I won't be long."

On the interstate, speeding toward his house, it struck him: Rachel had said "home." Ever since he had moved into a furnished studio apartment, Jeff always knocked on the front door when he picked up the kids. But today he let himself in with his key. From the living room, he heard Rachel call, "We're in here."

"I was just telling your wife I wouldn't be too worried," the police officer said. "Nine times out of ten, kids are off at the mall, or at a friend's house."

"They're only ten and twelve," Rachel said.

"They're skipping school younger and younger, ma'am. Even the good ones," the officer said, flipping the page in her notebook. "Let's see, what about family problems? Any, uh, issues between you two, or you and the kids?"

"We separated this summer," Rachel said.

Jeff glanced at Rachel's left hand. When had she stopped wearing her wedding band? "Will and Katie seem fine about it," he said.

The cop looked at Rachel. "They weren't happy about Thanksgiving," she said.

"I was going to take the kids to my mother's farm," Jeff told the officer. "Something came up at work."

"They were very excited about the trip," Rachel said.

"I had a deadline," Jeff said. "They understood."

"They were very disappointed," Rachel countered. "Especially Will."

"Come on, that's not fair," Jeff said, looking Rachel in the eye for the first time. "Will told me himself he thought he'd be bored out of his mind."

"What do you think he's going to say, Jeff? He was crushed."

The officer tapped the notebook against her chin. "Could they have gone there?"

Jeff shook his head. "Just a minute," Rachel said, and walked out of the room.

"Where does your mother live, Mr. Henderson?"

"Tennyson," Jeff said. "It's a small town, about five hours west of the city. No, it's too far." He looked at his watch: He was running out of time.

"Jeff!" Rachel stood at the top of the stairs, holding the piggy bank they had given Will last Christmas.

"It's empty," she said.

CHAPTER 2

Found and Lost

ome on, Mom. Pick up," Jeff said into the receiver as he listened to the phone ring again and again.

He imagined his mother drying her hands on the red-checked dish towel draped over the refrigerator handle, checking the gas burners on the stove, then walking through the dining room and into the front hall where a new phone rested on the oval table where a black rotary model had sat for forty years.

"I get her a portable so she can carry it with her," he said to the police officer. "So what does she do? She leaves it in the cradle. That's it; I'm buying her a phone for every room—and one for the barn, too. Ah, finally! Mom, are the kids there?"

Jeff gave a thumbs-up. Rachel sighed in relief, and the cop folded her notebook. But Jeff's mouth tightened as he listened.

"Why didn't you call to let us know? We were scared to death. Rachel called the police," he said. "No, Mom, we didn't put them on the bus. Let me talk to Will." He lowered the receiver and thanked the police officer. Rachel saw her to the door.

"What do you mean he doesn't want to talk to me? You tell him he's in big trouble if he doesn't get to the phone." Rachel tapped Jeff on the shoulder, and held out her hand. He gave her the phone, and smelled her hair's lemony scent.

Knowing her kids were safe transformed Rachel. She chatted with Jeff's mother, her tone changing only slightly when Will got on the phone.

It always amazed Jeff how Rachel was able to control her temper, even when the children pulled a stunt like this. Will talked to her because he knew his mother wouldn't jump down his throat.

Jeff held out his hand, and motioned for the phone; he would try her approach.

"It's okay, son. I'm not mad. I love you, and I'm glad you and your sister are safe," he said. "No, I don't know what we're going to do yet, but your mother and I will figure out something. Tell Katie I love her."

Jeff hung up, but before he could say a word, Rachel said, "The answer is no."

"Rachel, please. I'm in a jam. I've got to finish this report tonight."

"I'm sorry, Jeff, but I've made plans for the holidays. We agreed you'd have the kids for Thanksgiving, whether or not you went to your mother's."

Plans? he thought. With who?

"Fine then," he said. "They can just stay with my mom in Tennyson. I'll drive down on Thanksgiving."

"Jeff, they missed school today; they have one more day before Thanksgiving, and they're not missing it. If you leave now, you can make it back by morning. They can sleep in the car."

From the familiar chill in her voice, he knew she wouldn't relent; fifteen years of marriage had a way of teaching you the signs, even when the most important signals passed you by. He was going to Tennyson after all.

"Okay, Rachel, you win. Would you at least call and tell them I'm coming?"

"I'll be happy to. Now don't drive and talk on the phone. It's dangerous."

But Jeff was already heading out the door, punching auto dial for the office.

"Cheryl, something's come up with the kids," he said, backing out of the driveway and turning toward the interstate. "They're fine. But I'm not going to make it back in today. No, you don't have to get Susan, or anyone else, to fill in. And don't tell the big guy. Here's what I want you to do. E-mail me those spreadsheets. Thanks, you're a lifesaver."

He spotted a 7-Eleven; he'd need fortification.

"Oh, one more thing. Rachel's going out of town for the holiday and I forgot to get the number where she's staying. Can you call her and e-mail it, too?"

He filled up the gas tank and got a jumbo coffee. He had five hours of driving ahead of him. Five hours to unplug. No meetings, no e-mail, no voice mail messages. Five hours alone. Enough time, perhaps, to figure out why his wife and children were slipping from his grasp and what, if anything, he could do to keep from losing them forever.

CHAPTER 3

Homecoming

Fueled by twenty-four ounces of convenience-store coffee, Jeff zoomed along the interstate, bound for the farm town where he grew up.

Halfway there, snowflakes began speckling the windshield and the November day edged into night. He switched on the wipers and headlights, and scanned the radio for the weather.

With luck, and his radar detector, he would scoop up Will and Katie, and get home in time to make his deadline.

Unless.

The kids put up a fuss.

His mother guilt-tripped him into staying.

Or the forecaster—"Storm warning in effect. . . . Heavy snow expected over the next twenty-four hours"—was right. He could beat the storm and promise a longer Christmas visit. But if the kids started whining, all bets were off. He'd have to put his foot down, and once again, he'd be the heavy. Rachel would brush aside their protests, bundle them into the car and, only then, calmly inquire why they had done something as stupid and thoughtless as cutting school and taking a bus to Tennyson. No, she'd leave out the "stupid and thoughtless."

Even before the separation, Jeff knew his relationship with the kids wasn't as strong as Rachel's. But wasn't that because she spent more time with them while he was focused on work, providing for them? It wasn't his fault, it was the job—oh gosh, how was he going to get that report done if he couldn't make it back?

The snow thickened. Traffic slowed. Jeff notched up the wipers. He'd left behind the congestion of the city and the suburbs and now, on both sides, countryside spread toward a horizon bordered by the silhouette of skeletal trees.

WILFORD NEXT THREE EXITS, a roadside sign announced. Tennyson was too tiny for its own marker, but Jeff knew it was just twenty miles farther.

Up ahead, three lanes of traffic merged into a single scarlet procession of taillights, funneled by a police cruiser's flashers. Jeff hammered the steering wheel with his fist.

He crawled along until he came within earshot of a trooper in yellow rain gear, waving a flashlight. He lowered his window. Wind-driven snow stung his cheeks.

"What's the problem, officer?" Jeff called.

"Truck jackknifed five miles up."

"I'm trying to get to Tennyson," he said. "Any idea how long it's going to be?"

"No idea, sir. If I were you, I'd get off at the next exit. Second light, pick up State Road 9 West. Takes you right into Tennyson. It's longer," he said, shaking his head. "But tonight, it might get you there quicker. Besides," the trooper grinned. "It's the scenic route."

Jeff rolled his eyes. "Just what I need."

He couldn't remember the last time he'd driven along this winding two-lane road, still fringed with farms, fields, and woodlands. But when he was a kid—somewhere around Will's, or was it Katie's, age?—Route 9's black-top transported him and Pop, his grandfather, on their rounds at this very time of year. Rattling from farm to farm, they filled the pickup with Christmas wreaths, the season's last cash crop, which the farmers fashioned with holly boughs cut from the trees on their land. From his warehouse in town, Pop shipped them around the country for city folks to hang on their doors.

"Christmas from the forest," Pop called it. His name was Eben Henderson, but in these parts, everyone knew him as the Holly Wreath Man.

Those weren't easy days, especially—when was it, 1962?—when the world teetered on the brink of nuclear war, his grandfather's wreath business and health were failing, and Jeff's widowed mother, Allie, was on the verge of marrying a man she didn't love.

Still, to Jeff, turning into the driveway of the family farm, his life back then seemed far less complicated than today. Smoke plumed from the chimney, drifting over the barn behind it. Gravel crunched under the tires as he pulled up to the front porch.

The front door swung open, spilling light and a little girl who ran down the steps. His mother and Will followed.

"Daddy," Katie cried. "It's snowing!" Jeff breathed in the tang of wood smoke. He scooped up his daughter in one arm and hugged his mother with the other. Over her shoulder, he watched his son beeline away.

"Hey, Will!" Jeff called. The boy disappeared into the barn's shadow.

Jeff wished Pop was still alive. If anyone could help him out of the mess he'd made of his life, it was the Holly Wreath Man.

CHAPTER 4

Snowed In

D ad, you're not listening."

Jeff looked up from his laptop. "Katie, I'm trying to get online."

Jeff had retreated to the hallway, tethering his computer to the only phone line in the farmhouse. The modem's beeps and wheezes signaled his connection to the outside world.

"Yes!" he said. He turned to Katie, perched beside her grandmother on the living room sofa, a photo album open on her lap.

"I'm sorry we came to Tennyson without telling you or Mom," she said. "But now that we're here, could we ple-e-e-ze stay and go sledding tomorrow? Grandma says there's a Frequent Flyer sled in the barn."

"That's Flexible Flyer, honey," Jeff laughed. "Tell you what, Katie. Let me finish my work tonight. You and your brother get to bed. In the morning, if we have time, I'll give you fifteen minutes."

"That's bogus." Will, his cheeks pink with cold, protested from the kitchen doorway. Jeff had wondered how long it would take his son to come in from the cold.

"What's the rush, Jeff?" his mother said.

"Mom, I told you. I've got a very important meeting tomorrow." He stared pointedly at Will. "And these kids have school."

His mother looked out the window at the falling snow. "Your daddy's an optimist," she said. "If Grandpa can't make it home tonight from Wilford, you guys aren't going anywhere."

"Snowed in," Katie breathed.

Will nodded. "No school."

"Don't get their hopes up." Jeff loosened his tie, unbuttoned his collar. "I've got to get out of this suit," he said, heading upstairs. When he came back down, the kids burst out laughing. He had traded his suit for a pair of their grandfather's well-worn overalls, but was still wearing his dress shirt and tassel loafers.

He was heading back to his computer when the lights flickered and went out.

By an oil lamp's hazy light, Jeff watched his laptop dim and go dark. He slammed his cell phone shut. "No power. No battery. Out of range. Terrific."

"I'm not the one," his mother said, "who replaced our perfectly good phone with one that had to be plugged in. Just relax, Jeff." She patted the sofa. "Come down memory lane with us."

"Look at this wreath. It's bigger than Grandma and Grandpa," Katie said.

"That's the Radio City wreath," Jeff said.

"Who's the old guy with them?" Will asked.

"That's Pop. My grandfather," Jeff said. "Wasn't that the year I saw the Rockettes show, Mom?"

"That's right. 1962. We were lucky to make it that year," she said.

"Grandma, you're so pretty!" Katie said. "And Grandpa was handsome."

"He still is, as far I'm concerned." She snapped her fingers. "You know what? My stove's not electric. Who wants hot chocolate?"

"Me! Me!" the kids said.

"I've got leftover biscuits, too. All we need is some peach preserves to go with them. You boys fetch a jar from the root cellar."

Jeff led the way with a flashlight, grateful his mother had given him an opening with Will. One of his slick-soled loafers skidded on a cellar step.

"Careful, Dad," Will said.

"I'm okay," Jeff said. "Thanks."

Jars of fruit, preserves, and canned vegetables, as well as stacks of old magazines crowded the shelves.

Jeff waved the flashlight across them, bent down, and picked up a copy of *Life*, dated November 9, 1962. He brushed the magazine off on his overalls. "Oh boy, this takes me back."

Will read the headline out loud. "'Dealing with the Deadly Crisis, the

U.S. and Its People Withstand the Nuclear Threat,'" he said. "Dad, what's that mean?"

"The Cuban Missile Crisis. We thought Castro was going to blow up the world. Talk about scared." Jeff roamed the cellar with the flashlight. "I tried to turn this place into a fallout shelter. I was almost your age."

"Cool," Will said.

"Not at the time, believe me."

Jeff put the magazine under his arm, plucked a jar labeled PEACH and handed Will the flashlight. "Lead the way," he said.

Jeff was on the top step when he slipped again. This time, he lost his balance and tumbled backward into the darkness.

CHAPTER 5

The Show Starts

I'm okay, really," Jeff insisted. His mother lifted the ice pack off the bump on his head. "See, no blood," he told his kids, clustered around him at the kitchen table. He felt a little guilty that the worried look on Will's face pleased him.

Jeff picked up the *Life* magazine he'd brought upstairs and stood up. "I'm calling it a night."

"No biscuits, Dad?" Will said.

"I'll have mine in the morning. You two finish up and go to bed. If it stops snowing, we're leaving Tennyson. Early."

He kissed Katie and his mother. Will surprised him with a hug.

Jeff's upstairs bedroom hadn't changed much over the years. A shelf lined with Hardy Boy mysteries and baseball trophies decorated one wall. Over the single bed hung a Yankees pennant and a poster of the Radio City

Rockettes in red short-skirted Santa costumes. He kicked off his loafers, climbed under the chenille spread, and opened the yellowed magazine. In a mattress ad a woman slept alone in a double bed, her husband and son in the background. Where was Rachel sleeping tonight?

He turned the page. Fidel Castro's bearded face floated on the waves off a Havana beach. The picture was out of focus. Was it the camera or his vision?

Before Jeff could decide, he was out.

Inside Radio City Music Hall, a boy strolls through the Rockettes' dressing room. A leggy Rockette, dressed in a skimpy Santa costume trimmed with white fur, beckons.

"The show's about to begin," she whispers. "It can't start without you."

Jeff is dreaming, journeying back in time, his troubled soul searching for answers that could be found only in his past.

"Come on, Jeff. Jeffrey, wake up!" Allie Henderson, his mother, stood at the foot of his bed. The November 9, 1962, copy of *Life*, shiny and new, lay by his side. On the floor, a worn pair of PF Flyers rested on a heap of clothes. "You promised to help Pop with rounds before school. Don't keep him waiting."

Jeff Henderson was only ten, but his life on this November day in 1962 was full. Too full. And at the moment it was full of trouble.

He saw the worry on his mom's face—about the business, bills, and mostly, Pop's heart.

By now, a week before Thanksgiving, Pop's holly wreath business should be in full swing, holiday decorations flowing from his country warehouse to city department stores and nurseries. It wasn't.

By now, a month after the Cuban Missile Crisis had put America on high alert, the fallout shelter in the root cellar—Jeff's secret plan to save his mother and grandfather from the bomb—should have been chock-full of supplies. It wasn't.

A comforting morning smell—coffee, bacon, and biscuits—wafted up the stairs.

"Coming," Jeff said, rubbing his eyes.

Pop parked in front of a ramshackle farmhouse. Rusting machinery littered the front yard. The only bright note: holly wreaths stacked on two broomstick handles nailed to wooden bases.

A little girl peeked out the door. "Mommy, it's the Holly Wreath Man."

A tired-looking woman emerged, a toddler in her arms.

"I was hoping to have four sticks today, Pop, but Sammy's got croup again," she apologized. The baby barked a raspy cough.

Pop motioned to Jeff to start loading. "This is just fine," Pop said. "To tell the truth, Tammy, I'll be lucky to sell these two today."

"Come on, Pop," Tammy said. "You're kidding, right?"

"Fact is, demand's just not as strong this year."

"But Pop," Jeff said, "everybody needs a Christmas wreath, don't they?"

"Sure, son, but plastic seems to be the thing people want now."

"Who'd want plastic over a real one?" Tammy said.

"I've been asking myself the same question," Pop said.

"We're counting on our wreath money this year, what with the poor harvest and all," Tammy said anxiously. "I was planning on getting another four sticks done by Friday."

Tammy's husband pushed open the door, bleary-eyed, unshaven. "Think you could make any more noise out here?" he growled. "I'm trying to sleep."

Tammy reddened with embarrassment. "Sorry, hon. I was just telling Pop how we really need to sell a lot of wreaths this year."

"I'm tired of stepping on those stinking berries." He slammed the door.

Pop patted Tammy's shoulder. "Don't you worry. Make as many as you can. I'll take these up to Wilford today. People love Christmas from the forest, right, Jeff?"

Jeff grabbed the second stick of wreaths and headed for the truck. "You bet, Pop."

The truck loaded, Pop drove Jeff to school. At the warehouse, he hauled Tammy's wreaths up to the loading dock, stopping to catch his breath. He unlocked a side door, walked inside, and switched on the lights. Holly wreaths, in varying stages of decay, jammed the space. With a sigh, Pop added Tammy's wreaths to the pile, and locked up.

CHAPTER 6

The Thief

Y ou know it's just a matter of time," Jeff said, "before the Russians drop the bomb."

Randall Peterson, his best friend, removed a newspaper from the canvas sack hanging off his shoulder and lobbed the afternoon *Chronicle* onto Mrs. Waite's front porch. "They're sure not going to drop it on Tennyson. I don't know what you're so worried about."

"Because you can bet they're gonna drop one on Wilford Air Force Base. We'll get fallout from that, dumbbell."

"You're full of it."

"Yeah?" Jeff countered. "Well, President Kennedy isn't."

Randall stuffed a paper into the Brittinghams' mailbox.

"My dad says, 'A bomb's got your name on it, ain't nothing you can do about it.'"

"When the bomb turns your family into french fries, don't say I didn't warn you."

"Gross. I'd never say that about your family."

"You can't. We'll be in our bomb shelter."

"Root cellar, you mean."

Randall hit the Millers' front door with a *Chronicle*.

"Not for long." Jeff punched Randall's arm.

"Ouch! Watch my throwing arm."

The boys sauntered along Main Street. Jeff transferred Randall's now-empty bag to his own shoulder.

"What gives?" Randall said.

"Nothing. Just seeing what it feels like."

Randall shrugged. "You never want to carry it when there's papers in it."

Jeff halted in front of Swiggett's. "Let's see if the new *Superman*'s in."

Norman Rockwell could have painted Swiggett's General Store, a white clapboard building with a single gas pump out front. Inside, in the corner near the cash register, was a potbellied stove, brass spittoon, and a circle of cane chairs where white-haired regulars swapped tales. In back, beyond the dairy locker, a stairway led to Fred Swiggett's mezzanine office, which featured a special window: a one-way mirror. When he turned out his office light, people in the store saw only their reflections, unaware Fred could watch their every move.

Jeff held the door for a customer carrying a bag of groceries and a plastic Christmas wreath. Inside, he stopped at a display of artificial decorations by the cash register, a puzzled frown on his face.

"Hey, Mabel," he greeted the cashier. "Aren't you selling any of Pop's wreaths?"

Mabel looked up from the new *Photoplay*. "Sure, hon. Fred's keeping them in the dairy freezer, so they stay fresh."

"Oh," Jeff said. "Is he around?"

"No, hon. Fred's gone up to Wilford."

Seeing the boys head for the comics, she warned, "Don't bend the pages now. You know how he gets."

Jeff left Randall reading *Batman* and headed down the canned goods aisle. Keeping his back to Mabel, he flicked a can of pears into the sack, then a can of beans, and turned the corner into baking goods.

The front door opened and Fred Swiggett entered, carrying a stack of mail.

"Mabel, what'd I say about reading the merchandise?"

In front of the sugar display, Jeff froze.

Fred stopped at the cash register and handed her a manila envelope. "It's the Labor Department's new minimum wage poster. Put it up out back."

"Where?"

"I don't care. By the dairy locker's fine. I'll be in my office," Fred said. Jeff heard Fred's footsteps in the next aisle. He swiped a sack of sugar into the bag, just as Fred rounded the corner.

"Hey, boy," Fred said, "What you up to?"

"Nothing."

Fred eyed the newspaper bag. "I thought you were working with Pop."

Jeff clamped the sack shut. "I'm helping Randall today." After an awkward silence, he said, "So, you taking my mom out tonight?"

"I might be," Fred said, smoothing back his hair. Walking on, he said over his shoulder, "Stay out of trouble, hear?"

Outside the store, Randall retrieved his sack. Surprised by the weight, he looked inside. "What the heck is this? You didn't buy this stuff."

"So?"

"That's stealing, Jeff. Are you nuts?"

"No," Jeff whispered. "It's for the fallout shelter. You need at least enough food for a month." He pulled Randall into the alley alongside Swiggett's. "I've been taking food from home, but my mom's getting suspicious," he said, reaching into the bag.

Jeff plucked out the cans and put them in the pockets of his jacket. "Once my mom marries Fred, everything in the store will be ours anyway," he said, sounding like he was trying to convince himself. He zipped the sugar inside the front, securing the booty by folding his arms across his waist.

"I still think you're crazy."

"Just keep your mouth shut."

Randall snorted. "You think I want people knowing my best friend's a thief?"

CHAPTER 7

Proposal

Swiggett's General Store was dark, except for a single bank of lights over the meat counter.

"I want to show you something," Fred said, pulling Allie into the dairy locker, a chilled paneled room sealed with a heavy door.

"Very funny. It's freezing in here," she said.

"Wait," Fred said. He dragged a stack of milk crates from the wall, revealing an object covered with a tarp. "Ta-da!" he said dramatically, and whipped off the cover, unveiling a long rectangular sign emblazoned with SWIGGETT'S SUPERETTE in red, white, and blue letters.

"Well?" Fred demanded.

"Well, what?" Allie said.

"What do you think?"

"It's a sign," she said.

"A sign? It's a heck of a lot more than that. Look," he said, pointing at it. "Superette. No more General Store. We're moving into the modern age. Finally."

"That's nice," Allie said.

"Hey, what's with you tonight?"

"I told you. It's cold in here," she said. She shook her head. "Oh nothing, I'm sorry. I'm having trouble with Jeff."

Fred lifted his eyebrows in an I-told-you-so arch and said, "He needs a man around the house."

"He's got Pop."

"Pop's an old man. Jeff needs a father figure, a man he can look up to."

"And that, I suppose, is you?"

"None other," Fred said, slicking back his hair.

Fred wrapped his arms around Allie. "So what do you say?" he said, nuzzling her neck. "Let's make it official. Tonight."

Allie twisted out of his grasp. "Fred, please," she said. "I want to get out of here. I'm cold. And I've told you before, I can't make any decisions during holly season." She headed for the door. Catching sight of the holly wreaths piled on the floor, she stopped.

"Are these Pop's wreaths? Fred, what are they doing back here?"

"Oh, for crying out loud, Allie. There is no more wreath season. Pop doesn't want to accept that. Neither do you. But that's the truth. How many buyers does Pop have?"

"I don't know. The usual."

"No, not anymore. The big stores are selling plastic wreaths."

"That may be so, but there are still people who like the natural way," she said. "And Radio City still wants its big wreath. That hasn't changed."

"Yeah? Who's going to make it? People aren't going to do it for nothin.' It's the '60s, Allie. People expect to get paid a decent wage." He stopped. "Does Pop even pay minimum wage?"

She shrugged. "Everyone knows you don't get rich making wreaths."

"Exactly my point. You're wasting your time. You know what?" he said, his eyes lighting with excitement, "Come work here. Mabel's not worth the money I pay her. Now, you and I, we'd make a great team."

"Fred, you don't listen," she said, crossing her arms and hugging herself.

"Allie, come on," Fred interrupted. "You're the one not listening. I can't even sell any of the darn things."

She bent down, picked up a wreath, and held it up to his face. "Maybe people would buy them if you put them out in the store instead of burying them back here."

"Allie, if it'll make you feel better, I'll put some out right now."

"Fred, don't do us any favors," she said, handing him the wreath. "I told you, I'm cold. I want to go home. Now." She walked out of the dairy locker and into the store.

Fred shook his head and dropped the wreath back on the pile. He paused to admire his sign, and replaced the tarp and crates that concealed it. He left the locker, angrily slamming the door shut behind him. A sign posted on the wall fluttered to the floor. Cursing, Fred bent down to pick it up, and read the boldfaced type: YOUR RIGHTS UNDER THE FAIR LABOR STANDARDS ACT. FEDERAL MINIMUM WAGE. $1.15 AN HOUR, EFFECTIVE SEPT. 1, 1961. $1.25 AN HOUR EFFECTIVE SEPT. 1, 1963.

"That Mabel! Can't even hang up a sign right," he muttered. "And I've got to give her a raise next year?" He pressed the sign back onto the wall.

"Fred!" Allie called impatiently. He gazed out toward the store, looked back at the poster and studied it, running his finger down the page until he reached a line that said, FOR ADDITIONAL INFORMATION, CONTACT THE WAGE AND HOUR DIVISION OFFICE NEAREST YOU.

Fred smoothed back his hair, a smile spreading across his face. "Here I come, darlin'."

CHAPTER 8

Betrayal

Ever so carefully, Fred pulled up to the back of his store in the 1962 Ford Galaxie convertible, Corinthian white with red trim, that was his pride and joy. He spied a smudge, took out his handkerchief, and gently rubbed it clean. Satisfied, he opened the store's back door and quietly made his way to his upstairs office. For the job he had to do, he didn't want any interruptions.

Fred loved his office, just big enough for a desk facing the one-way mirror that gave him a bird's-eye view of his domain. It was slow, only Mabel at her register and two old cronies by the stove.

He opened the phone book. Turning on the desk lamp would give him away, but enough light streamed in from the store for him to read the number for the Wage and Hour Division.

The world was changing, leaving the old ways and old-timers like Pop behind, Fred thought as he dialed. Allie's future lay with him and the Superette, not with holly wreaths nobody wanted anymore. She just needed a little push to see it.

"If you look into it," Fred said, "you'll find that Henderson doesn't pay minimum wage to those farmers who make his wreaths." He paused and looked out the mirror just in time to see Jeff Henderson, in canned goods, appear to slip something into his jacket pocket.

Fred leaped to his feet. "Look, your investigator won't have any trouble finding him," he said.

Jeff moved down to the spice rack, looked over each shoulder, and lifted a jar in each hand.

"Just tell him to ask for the Holly Wreath Man," continued Fred, dragging the phone across the desk.

He was about to bang on the glass when a customer crossed over into Jeff's aisle. The boy returned the jars and hurried out, leaving Fred with nothing but his suspicions.

Fred scowled. "Just say I'm a concerned businessman who believes in the Fair Labor Standards Act."

Fred hung up the phone, switched on the light, and smoothed back his hair.

The next morning, the usual collection of pickups, station wagons, and delivery vans jammed the Farmers Market parking lot on the banks of the Wilford River. Inside, buyers and sellers filled the cavernous space with tobacco smoke and the din of bartering.

Pop Henderson stood at a table stacked with holly wreaths, arguing with a department store buyer.

"You've seen this coming for years, Eben. The market's just not there anymore," the buyer said, brushing dust from his overcoat. "People want things they can pack away and use next year."

Two hundred miles away, on a city street flanked by brick factories, Labor Department investigator John Turner sat in a gray sedan watching women bundled against the autumn cold scurry inside the employee entrance of Marvella Fashions.

The *Chronicle* spread across the steering wheel gave cover for the notepad where Turner counted the employees disappearing inside the factory. The sidewalk cleared. He checked his watch—8:02 a.m.—and tallied the numbers, writing "65" in an angry slash at the bottom of the page.

A gleaming 1963 Cadillac pulled into a space with the name MR. HORTON stenciled on the wall. A tall man in a camel hair topcoat got out. Turner crossed the street, limping slightly.

"I have nothing to say to you," Horton shouted, edging fearfully toward the door as Turner approached. "I told you yesterday, talk to my attorney."

Turner stopped at the Cadillac's rear fin. "I just have one question for you, Horton."

"What?" Horton said, suspiciously.

Turner sauntered around the car, his hand caressing the tail fin.

"Yesterday your books showed thirty-five workers on the day shift."

"So?"

"So how come I count sixty-five going in today?"

Horton blanched. "Like I said, Turner, talk to my attorney."

Turner grasped Horton's lapel, leaned into his face, and said, "I'm going to shut you down."

"Get your hands off me!" Horton cried, breaking away. He dashed to the door, looked back to see if Turner followed, and ran inside.

Turner rubbed his fingers and said, almost wistfully, "Nice coat."

At noon, Pop stood on the Wilford River Bridge, staring at the water below. He stepped back and reached into the pickup bed full of wreaths and began tossing them over the rail. They sailed through the air, landed with tiny splashes, and in the gentle current, floated away.

CHAPTER 9

An Honest Man

Stakeouts didn't always pan out. Paper trails went cold. Numbers didn't add up. To take down crooked employers, John Turner had to reach out to those who had the most to lose: exploited workers whose meager paychecks were better than none.

"Excuse me, ladies." Turner stood in the windowless room where Marvella Fashions' seamstresses ate lunch. "I'm with the U.S. Labor Department. I'm investigating complaints that your employer doesn't pay minimum wage, as required by federal law."

The women exchanged puzzled looks and whispers. He opened his wallet, revealing his badge. Their confusion turned to fear, and the room echoed with the same word in several languages: *"Policia! Polizia! Policias! Policja!"*

"No police. Labor Department. Here to help you." But the room emptied as the women gathered up their lunches, brushing past Horton and his foreman, who'd come to the doorway.

"You got everything the other day. You're harassing my workers and interfering with my constitutional rights," Horton said.

"To do what?" Turner said. "Cheat people?"

"I pay minimum wage. Ask anybody. Right, Joe?" Horton said.

The foreman's eyes took on a deer-in-the-headlights glaze. "Sure, sure, minimum wage."

"Right," Turner said, turning to leave, then swiveling back. "Say Joe, what is minimum wage?"

Eyeing the boss, Joe stammered, "Uh, seventy-five cents?"

Horton bit down on his cigar and gave his head a little shake.

"No, no, I know. A dollar." Horton's face darkened. A sheen of sweat glistened on Joe's brow. "I mean, a buck ten. Yeah, that's it."

"Close, Joe, but no cigar," Turner said, shouldering his way between the two men.

"Give it up, Turner. If you think any of my girls are going to talk to you, even if they could speak English, you're stupider than this moron," Horton said, jerking his finger at Joe.

Turner stopped, inches from Horton's face. "You're finished."

"Lay a hand on me, pal," Horton said, "and you're the one who's finished."

Turner brushed past the owner, walked down the hall and through the throng of women eating lunch in the stairwell. They rose, ready to bolt again. Turner raised his hands in a peacekeeping gesture. "Stay, stay."

How could he ever help them, he thought, if they didn't trust him?

Turner walked into the Capitol Diner and took a counter seat next to Peter Doyle, reporter for the *Chronicle*.

"Ah, the eternal cynic," Doyle said, raising his coffee cup. "How goes the search, Turner?"

Turner played along. "What search would that be?"

"Why, your continuing but fruitless quest for one honest man, my friend. Did you know, Mary," Doyle said, turning to the waitress, "Turner's a modern-day Diogenes?" Unimpressed, Mary kept wrapping silverware in white paper napkins.

Undeterred, Doyle continued. "Like our beloved Greek philosopher who prowled the wide world with his lantern, our man Turner scours the working world, ever vigilant, peering at the careworn faces of beleaguered bosses searching for that one honest soul. Pray, traveler, give us your report. Have you found a contender?"

"Just coffee, Mary. Thanks," Turner said. "Just left one who thinks he fits the description."

"The envelope, please." Doyle beat a drum roll on the counter. "And the winner is . . . ?"

"Danny Horton."

Doyle rolled his eyes, and continuing the charade, rubbed his chin and appeared to consider for a moment.

"Ah yes, Mr. Horton. I believe I covered his arraignment, let's see, five years ago? Yes, assault with intent to murder. I believe his defense was 'The poor victim had accidentally fallen from his car,' a turn of events that said victim eventually came to accept as accurate. Case dismissed."

"Yeah, well this time I'm nailing him," Turner said. He sipped his coffee. "So, smart guy, how did Diogenes make out? Did he ever find an honest man?"

"What do you think, Turner?"

Turner shook his head. "I don't think he did. There aren't any. At least, I sure haven't met one. I doubt I ever will."

"Turner, my friend, you are not alone," Doyle said. He raised his cup. "To the search."

At home in Tennyson that evening, Allie Henderson scanned the shelves of the kitchen cupboard. "I've looked everywhere," she said. "I must be losing my mind."

"Why's that?" Pop looked up from the apple he was peeling.

"I know I bought three cans of creamed corn last week," Allie said. "We had two for Sunday dinner. And now, for the life of me, I can't find the other one."

At the kitchen table, Jeff was the picture of innocence, but he stopped reading his magazine and listened, shoulders hunched, like a deer ready to bolt.

CHAPTER 10

Last Chance

I f I had my way, Turner, I'd fire you right now," said Raymond Metcalf, regional director of the Wage and Hour Division office. "You don't threaten employers."

"I didn't threaten anybody," Turner said.

"You didn't grab Danny Horton around the neck and tell him you were going to beat him up?"

"All I did was admire his coat," Turner said. "And tell him I'd shut him down."

"Well, you won't. You're off the case."

Turner jumped to his feet. "I've been working that case for six months."

"You're lucky Horton didn't have you arrested. I just spent the last hour talking his lawyer out of pressing assault charges."

"The guy's a crook," Turner said. "Who's running this office now, us or the sweatshop owners?"

"Listen, you idiot, shut up and sit down." Turner sat. "You're lucky Horton's lawyer called. I'm surprised you weren't found floating in the river."

Metcalf opened a folder on his desk. "I've been looking over your file, Turner. Very impressive, I must say." He turned a page. "When Washington transferred you here, I figured I must be doing something right to deserve such a hot shot.

"Let's see. Six years in the Manhattan office. Five convictions, $100,000 paid in back wages. Four years in Boston; string of good cases there. Two years in Providence. Pretty good record going after textile mills. Got your legs broken in the process."

"Glad to see you can read," Turner said.

"As I say, I was thrilled Washington sent you here, though I confess I was a bit curious why. Any ideas?"

Turner kept silent.

"You don't care much for paperwork, do you, Turner?" He started flipping pages rapidly. "Incomplete reports, reports never turned in. Chronic tardiness. Absent without leave. Harassment complaints."

Metcalf closed the folder and smacked it with an open palm. "You've got a problem, Turner. I don't know what it is, and frankly, I don't care. What I do care about is your performance in this office. And if that doesn't improve I can guarantee you one thing: You're out. I talked to Washington this morning. Personally, I think they're crazy. But they're willing to give you one more chance."

Metcalf opened the humidor on his desk and removed a cigar. He lit it with a flourish, puffing until the end glowed red and smoke wreathed his face.

"Let's see how you handle this new assignment." He picked up another folder and opened it.

"Not your normal minimum-wage violation, although it's appropriate for the season." Metcalf grinned, a frosty, mirthless smirk.

"Fellow named Henderson," he said, consulting the report. "Nursery operation, looks like. Hires local farmers to make Christmas wreaths and sells them nationwide to department stores. Does business as," he looked down, "the Holly Wreath Man."

"Sounds dangerous," Turner said sarcastically. "What city is he in?"

"No city."

"Suburbs?"

Metcalf was enjoying this. "He's located in Tennyson."

"Never heard of it," Turner said.

"I'm not surprised. It's downstate. About five hours from here."

"You're sending me to the boondocks? Listen, I'll take a suspension."

Metcalf leaned forward. "Turner, you don't get it. It's this, or nothing. Check out this Holly Wreath Man. If he's in violation, we'll shut him down." He leaned back and blew a smoke ring skyward. "Might make good news copy," he mused. "Labor Department rescues farmers." He leaned forward. "Any questions?"

"Just one," Turner said. "You pay for that cigar or pick it up off the sidewalk?"

"Enjoy the country, Turner."

At the Tennyson Post Office, Pop Henderson opened his mailbox. Empty. At the counter, Hank Pritchard paid for his stamps and followed him outside.

"Henderson," he called. "Hold up. Given my offer any more thought?" asked Pritchard, who was making a fortune turning downstate farms into subdivisions.

"Some," Pop said.

"I'd like to break ground this spring," he said, waiting for a response that didn't come. "This can mean a future for your family."

"That land is their future," Pop said.

"Not with holly trees on it. Put houses on it and you've got something. But if it's a nursery business you want, you'll have enough cash to open a greenhouse. Or a flower shop. That's a business for today. Weddings. Anniversaries. Funerals."

"The wreath business may not be what it used to," Pop said. "But I've still got customers and suppliers who depend on me."

Pritchard climbed into his pickup with his company logo painted on the passenger door: HOLLY ESTATES: LIVING AT ITS FINEST.

"For how long, Henderson?" he said. "That's the question."

CHAPTER 11

Dirt Poor

As the week's episode of *The Millionaire* came to a close, John Beresford Tipton, concealed in his leather chair, conferred with Michael Anthony, who would deliver the rich man's windfalls the next week. Allie switched off the TV, turned to Jeff and Pop, and launched the family's version of the popular show. "So, what would you do with a million dollars?"

"I always go first," Pop said. "Your turn, Allie."

She leaned back on the sofa. "First, I'd pay all the bills and the mortgage. I'd buy Jeff that three-speed bike, and Pop, I'd spruce up your office."

"Don't waste your money," Pop said.

"Things are just slow," she countered. "They'll pick up, the closer we get to Christmas. They always do."

Pop shrugged and said, "Jeff, you go."

Sitting on the rug, Jeff didn't turn around. "It's a stupid game."

"You always liked playing it before," his mother said, trading a surprised look with Pop.

"It's a TV show, Mom. Nobody's giving us a million dollars," Jeff said over his shoulder. "Face it, we're dirt poor and always will be," he said bitterly, running from the room.

Mystified, Allie said, "What's that all about?"

Pop stood up. "I'll talk to him." He found Jeff on the front-porch steps and sat down beside him. "Your Mom's worried about you, Jeff."

"It's nothing," Jeff said, staring at his sneakers. Pop waited. "It's just something one of the guys at school said."

"Yeah?"

"That we're dirt poor." They could see their breath in the night air.

"Hmm," Pop said, weighing the words. "Do you know what that means?"

"Yeah, that we don't have any money."

"That's one way to look at it, I guess," Pop said, cupping his chin.

"And that's what we are, isn't it, Pop?" Jeff demanded.

"Dirt's not poor," Pop said. He gestured at the fields. "How can it be poor if you can grow crops in it that feed an entire country?" His hand swept over the shadowy woods beyond. "And raise holly trees that help folks put food on the table and presents under the Christmas tree?"

He put his arm around Jeff and pulled him close. "Jeff, the way I see it, dirt may look poor, but it's rich. Rich with possibility. And as long as we have it, so are we."

Jeff nodded. "I guess you're right."

For a moment they sat in silence.

"Pop, are the Russians still in Cuba?" he said.

"I think so. Why do you ask?"

"We had another air-raid drill at school today. We're learning how to duck and cover."

"Well, I wouldn't worry too much. Kennedy got that Khrushchev fella to back down. It looks like it's blowing over."

"It doesn't hurt to be prepared though, right?"

"Course," Pop said. "Better safe than sorry."

"Well, that's good." Jeff shivered.

Pop got up. "Come on, let's get back inside before your mom thinks we've run off."

"Pop?"

"Yes, son."

A sly smile spread across Jeff's face. "So what would you do if you had a million dollars?"

"I got some things in mind. How about you?"

"Yeah," Jeff said. "Me, too."

The next morning, a gray sedan pulled up outside Pop's office. John Turner got out, took in the weather-beaten building, its small hand-painted sign advertising HOLLY WREATHS FOR SALE, and shook his head. He limped up the stairs and opened the door.

The old man on the phone waved him toward an empty chair.

"Bill's retired? Good for him. So who's the new nursery buyer?" Pop asked. "Arnold Sheckman?" He wrote the name down. "Could you put me through to him, please? Well, when he's out of his meeting, would you have him call me?"

Pop listened, and made a fist. "Of course, I could write a letter," he said angrily, and then took a deep breath. "But your order's usually in by now and I always spoke with Bill about this kind of thing." He listened again.

"Oh, I see, Mr. Sheckman prefers correspondence. Fine, I'll send him a letter then. But if he still could give me a call, I'd appreciate it. I'd just like to say hello. Hello? Hello? Miss? Hello?"

Turner cleared his throat. "Excuse me," he said. "I'm looking for the owner."

Pop hung up the phone. "You got him."

CHAPTER 12

The Country Code

Twenty years in the field had taught John Turner one indisputable fact: What sweatshop owners told you and what you found in their records were two entirely different things. He was certain that the Holly Wreath Man was no exception.

"My daddy started the business during the Depression. It was big business for a while," Pop Henderson said, pointing to a faded photo of a train bearing a HOLLY EXPRESS sign on a boxcar. "Back then, holly wreaths were the only way some of us made it through the winter."

"Interesting, I'm sure," said Turner. "But it's 1962. How does your business operate today?"

"Farmers, and some townsfolk, supply the wreaths. I supply the buyers," Pop said. "I'm just a middleman."

"No, Mr. Henderson, you're an employer," Turner said. He cursed

Metcalf, his boss, for wasting his time when he could be back in the city, closing the case on Danny Horton.

"Listen," he said, impatiently. "I've heard every excuse there is, so let's cut to the chase. Let me guess. You're not making money. Heck, your workers get more out of it than you do. Why, with your overhead you barely break even. That it?"

"In a nutshell," Pop said.

"Right. And if you had to pay minimum wage, you'd have to shut down."

"You really understand the way things work around here."

"You bet I do," Turner said, opening his notebook. "And that's why I want to see your payroll, timesheets, work schedules, all of it. Feel free to call your lawyer, but you'll hear the same: You have to comply."

Pop felt a familiar heartburn spread in his chest. "I've got nothing to hide," he protested. He sifted through piles of paper, but the mess stopped him. His hands shook. "I might need a little time. It's our busy season."

Turner got to his feet. "Well, while you're looking, I'd like to talk to some of your employees. Where can I find them?"

For the first time, Pop laughed. "Home, I'd imagine. They harvest the holly from trees on their land, make the wreaths, and I pick them up and ship them out from here. I'd be happy to take you out to meet the folks."

"That won't be necessary."

"I'm not going to put a spell on them. It's just, well, I don't think they'll talk to you."

"I don't think I'll have any trouble," Turner said.

The next few hours Turner drove up and down Route 9, stopping at farmhouses. The first farmer he asked for information went back inside and returned with a shotgun that he leveled at Turner.

"Off my land."

At the next stop, the farmer looked up from the tractor engine he was working on.

"That's a rude question to ask a friend, let alone a stranger. How much do you make, mister? Whatever it is, you're overpaid."

At the third house, a farm wife turned on her heel without a word. Henderson must have called ahead. Turner got behind the wheel and pulled away in a cloud of dust.

Dwarfed by a pile of holly sprays on her kitchen table, Olivia Coffin, a heavyset woman in her eighties, surprised Turner with a friendly welcome.

"Can't stop working, sonny. Start talking."

"How much do you get paid?"

"That depends," she said, joining two boughs of gleaming holly with a length of baling wire.

"On what?"

"How much work I do, of course."

"Well, how much do you get paid an hour?"

"That depends."

"On what?"

"How much I do."

"Well, how much do you do? Don't tell me," he said, closing his notebook. "That depends."

"You're catching on."

Pop looked up from the ledger open on his desk. The pain in his chest had migrated to his left arm. He opened the desk drawer, fished out a business card, and picked up the phone.

"Pritchard, I've changed my mind about the land," he said. "I'm ready to sell."

He heard a clatter on the stairs and hung up as Jeff burst in the door.

"Pop, where have you been?" he said, out of breath. "I've been waiting for you since school got out. I thought we were collecting wreaths today?"

"Been a bit tied up, son," Pop said, wincing in pain.

"Pop, are you okay?" Jeff said, alarmed by his grandfather's ashen face.

Inside Pop's chest, a burning fist squeezed. Tighter. And tighter. He tried to stand up, but fell back in the chair and reached helplessly for the phone.

"Jeff," he gasped. "Call your mom."

CHAPTER 13

Pop's Secret

At Wilford Memorial Hospital, Pop lay on a gurney in the emergency room.

"This is a lot of foolishness," he insisted to Allie and Jeff, standing on either side. "I'm telling you, I'm fine."

"Maybe so, Pop," said Allie. "Your color is better." She brushed his snowy hair off his forehead. "But let's hear what the doctor says."

"Why?" said Dr. Quillen, opening the curtain and picking up the chart clipped to the end of the gurney. "He's never listened before."

"Hogwash," Pop muttered. Quillen was Tennyson's family doctor, the man who'd cared for Pop and his kin all their lives.

"Don't give me that, Eben. I've told you a hundred times you need to take it easy. Neither of us is getting any younger."

"Speak for yourself, sawbones." They grinned at each other.

"Did Pop have a heart attack?" Jeff said.

"I don't think so, son. His EKG was normal. I want to run some more tests."

Pop raised his arm in protest.

"That's right, my friend. You're spending the night." Quillen took Pop's pulse. "It's not unusual for other things to cause chest pain. You said this happened after lunch?"

Jeff nodded. "Yes, sir."

"If I were a betting man, I'd say it's a stomach ulcer. The symptoms mimic angina pectoris. But we'll know more tomorrow. In the meantime, my friend, you need to lie back and relax."

"Relax? Listen, you old quack, Christmas is around the corner, my busiest time." Pop tried to get up. "Just give me some antacid pills and let me get out of here."

Dr. Quillen rested his hand on Pop's shoulder and gently pressed back. "All right, now. That's about it. You're going to give Allie and Jeff here a heart attack. Now it might be heartburn, but it might be something more serious. One thing's for certain. Stress is not going to help. You need to rest. That's an order. For once, you stubborn old fool, do what you're told."

"Don't you worry, doctor," Allie said firmly. "He's going to get lots of rest. I'll see to that." She squeezed Pop's hand. "I can take care of things. And Jeff will help."

"Mom's right, Pop," the boy piped up. "We can pick up the wreaths from

Mrs. Coffin and Miss Tammy, everybody's. You just take care of yourself."

"Jeff, I know you can," Pop said, grasping the boy's hand. He teared up and coughed.

"You, young man, are going home to finish your homework," his mother said. "I'll go to the office and look over the books."

"But I have a system," Pop protested. "You'll never figure it out."

Allie gave him an affectionate smile. "Pop, I can add and subtract, okay? We'll do fine. You just rest."

Allie gazed at two framed pictures on Pop's overflowing desk. The first was taken in 1952 just before Bobby, her husband, shipped out to Korea. He looked so young in his marine uniform, standing between Pop and Allie. She was pregnant with the son Bobby would never hold. In the other photo, a crowd of farmers gathered around a truck, Pop at the wheel, a huge wreath in back, and, stretched across the side, a banner proclaiming RADIO CITY MUSIC HALL OR BUST! From under a pile of invoices, she pulled out Pop's ledger.

Something didn't add up. The first time Allie totaled the season's receipts in Pop's ledger, she figured she had made a mistake. So she did it again. And then, with a sinking feeling growing in the pit of her stomach, she ran the figures through Pop's old adding machine one more time. The money coming in from buyers didn't match the amount Pop was paying the farmers who supplied the wreaths. And he hadn't made any entries, it seemed, in weeks. How could that be?

She lifted piles of paper, rooted through the desk drawer. Nothing there but letters and a shiny new key. Maybe there were invoices in the storage room next door.

Allie stood before the storage room door, staring at a padlock, shiny and new, like that key. Pop had never locked anything before. Why now?

She went back and got the key. It fit, and Allie opened the door. Even before she turned on the light, the pungent smell of decaying leaves revealed Pop's secret. Allie covered her mouth with her hand, her eyes filling with tears at the sight—stacks of unsold wreaths filled the room.

CHAPTER 14

Gotcha!

Fred Swiggett sat in his office flipping through inventory sheets when Jeff walked into the general store. Here was his chance. Fred grabbed his coat and hat and dashed downstairs.

"Mabel, I'm going over to Wilford for a couple of hours," he said, deliberately raising his voice. "I should be back by 5:30." He waved at Jeff, who stood by the magazines. "How's Pop feeling?"

"Better. He's coming home from the hospital tomorrow."

"Delighted to hear it," Fred said. "Your mama over at the hospital?"

"No," Jeff said. "She's at Pop's taking care of business."

Fred walked up to him. "And what are you up to?" he said, enjoying the look of panic flashing across the boy's face.

"Nothing. Just thought I'd come in and look at the magazines. Did the new *Life* come in, Miss Mabel?"

"Not yet, hon."

"Tell your mama I'll give her a call later," Fred said. He nodded to two old timers jawing by the stove and headed out the door.

"Sure," Jeff said.

Jeff watched Fred start up his car and drive away. Mabel opened her purse, pulled out an emery board, and began filing her nails.

Jeff put the comic book down and headed for the spice rack. He paused, scanning the selection, then pocketed a can of cinnamon and moved on to the soup aisle. He reached for Campbell's chicken noodle. A hand shot in front of him and grabbed his outstretched arm.

"Gotcha!" Fred said.

It had taken Allie most of the day, but Pop's desk hadn't been this clean in years. She'd tossed out piles of old newspapers and sorted leaning towers of invoices and bank statements.

With each mess tidied she felt more despondent. Fred was right; there was no holly wreath business anymore, at least not a profitable one. From the drawer where she'd found the storage room key, she now pulled out a handful of letters, and began to read.

"Dear Mr. Henderson, With the growing popularity of artificial decorations, Macy's demand for your product has been reduced. Thank you for your interest."

The letter was dated November 1960—two years ago.

Another began:

"Pop, I wish I could help, but the powers that be have decided against natural wreaths in favor of plastic. I don't agree, but have no say in the matter."

From one of his best customers, it had come in just a month ago.

The door opened. Allie hastily wiped her eyes. The thin, dark-haired man who walked in, limping slightly, seemed surprised to see her.

"Oh, excuse me," he said. "I'm looking for Mr. Henderson."

"He's not here. Do you want to place an order?"

"No," Turner smiled. "Do you know when he'll be back?"

"He won't. At least not for a while."

"That's convenient," Turner said.

"What did you say?" Allie said.

"I said, that's convenient." He paused. "Do you work for him?"

"I'm his daughter-in-law," Allie said, her face coloring. "Not that it's any of your business."

"I wouldn't be so sure, Miss . . . ?"

"Mrs. Henderson."

"Mrs. Henderson, didn't your father-in-law tell you about my visit?"

"No. Who are you?"

"The name's Turner. U.S. Labor Department," he said, producing his badge. "I'm investigating Mr. Henderson."

"For what?" Allie said, her voice rising. "What could he possibly have done?"

"For starters, not paying minimum wage."

"How could he? Do you know how much he pays for wreaths?"

"That's not the point, Mrs. Henderson. Like I told him, the law's the law."

"Wait a minute," Allie said, standing up. "When did you see him?"

"Just yesterday. I told him I'd need to see his books and talk to his employees, although they weren't much help."

"He's in the hospital," Allie shouted. "And you put him there! You want his books? Here." She picked up the ledger and threw it at him.

For once, Turner was speechless.

The phone rang.

"Hello. What!? He's where? Oh Fred, no." Allie hung up. "I've got to go."

"Look, I'm sorry for your trouble," Turner told her, turning to leave. "But this isn't going away."

Jeff sat on the top bunk in a basement holding cell at the Tennyson police station. He hugged his knees and shivered, trying to keep from crying and breathing in the sour smell rising from the man passed out on the bottom bunk.

CHAPTER 15

Fallout

The desk sergeant looked down at Allie from his elevated seat behind the counter.

"Don't worry, Allie. Fred's not pressing charges," he said. "He just wanted to put a scare into the boy. That's usually all it takes."

Allie and Jeff rode home in silence, passing the autumn landscape of brown fields and rich green stands of pine and holly. They rounded the bend on Route 9 and the farm came into view.

"Mom."

"I don't want to hear it."

"Let me explain."

"We'll talk inside." She turned into the driveway.

"You don't understand," Jeff said.

Allie braked suddenly, the truck skidding in the gravel. "Oh, I understand. You were caught stealing." She shifted into neutral and faced him. "How could you, Jeff? With Pop in the hospital, and me trying to keep the business going?"

"That's not fair," Jeff protested.

"Fair?" Allie shouted, losing her patience. She reached out to slap him, caught herself, and slammed her open palm against the steering wheel instead. Alarmed, Jeff jerked open the door and jumped from the cab. "I can show you. I can show you," he cried, running across the yard toward the back of the house.

"Jeff, get back here," she yelled. She cut the engine and ran after him.

Jeff rounded the house and pulled open the door that led into the cellar.

When Allie reached him, he was on the top step, tears running down his face.

"It was supposed to be a surprise."

"What was?"

"I'll show you, Mom." She followed him down into the darkness.

"I got the idea after President Kennedy said the Russians might bomb us from Cuba. I thought we'd be safe down here, you, Pop, me." He hesitated. "Fred, too. I figured since you were going to get married, taking the stuff from Swiggett's wasn't really stealing. I was wrong." He sniffled. "I'm sorry, Mom."

Jeff pulled on the light chain, the bare bulb's glare momentarily blinding her.

"I was trying to get enough stuff so we could stay down here a month, until it was safe. It was going to be my Christmas present to you and Pop."

He pulled a blanket away from the wall. Allie saw, neatly lined up on one shelf, a bag of sugar, cans of beans and pears, and the corn that had vanished the other day from the kitchen cupboard.

"I'm sorry, Mom," Jeff said. "I just don't want us to die."

"Oh, honey," she said, hugging him tightly.

Allie found Fred stacking empty milk crates behind the store. "Did you have to have him arrested?" she demanded.

"Allie, they just went through the motions at the police station. Do you think I'd want my stepson to have a police record?"

"But couldn't you have called me first? I was scared to death."

"The boy needed to be taught a lesson."

Allie sat cross-legged in front of her husband's grave. The small American flag left by the VFW fluttered in the wind. Whenever she was unsure of life or herself, she found comfort at the old Tennyson cemetery. She had to do something to stop her world from falling apart.

She couldn't disagree with Fred. She sat on the hard ground, weighing her happiness against her son's future, until the cold reached every part of her being, and she made her decision.

"Do you love him, Allie?" Pop said.

"Fred will be a good provider. And Jeff needs a father."

Pop pushed away the hospital tray of Jell-O, broth, and ginger ale. "If what ails you doesn't kill you, the food here will," he said disgustedly. "You didn't answer my question."

"Pop, I'm never going to find what Bobby and I had again."

"You never know," he said. She gazed out the window and then turned to him.

"Pop, I've got a question for you. Mind telling me about your plans for the wreaths in the locked storeroom?"

He didn't answer. "I've gone over the books," she said softly. "I read the letters from your buyers. Pop, why didn't you say anything?"

"How could I tell Tammy, Olivia—any of them—that nobody wants their wreaths anymore?" He shook his head. "I couldn't do it."

"But Pop, you don't have the money to pay them yourself," Allie said. "Maybe it's time to shut down."

"I don't have the heart to," he said. For a moment, they were both lost in thought.

"Pop?" Allie said. "Would you walk me down the aisle?"

"I'd be honored," he said, his voice cracking.

CHAPTER 16

Making the Case

For the fourth time that November day, Allie stood outside a holly wreath maker's home and said, "This is Mr. Turner of the Labor Department."

She hoped this was the right thing, introducing the investigator to Pop's suspicious suppliers. Pop was home from the hospital, but she knew he couldn't shut down the business on his own. Helping Turner might be the only way to keep Pop alive.

Tammy Lewis glared down from her porch, arms crossed. Her daughter peeked at the visitors from behind her mother's skirt.

"I heard all about him, Allie," she said. "I've got nothing to say."

"I'd just like to ask you a few questions," Turner said.

"What for?" Tammy said, eyeing his notebook. "To get Pop in trouble?"

"No, Tammy," Allie interrupted. "To get him out of trouble. Somebody told the government Pop wasn't doing right by his wreath makers."

"That's stupid," Tammy said indignantly. "If it wasn't for Pop, I don't know how we'd make it."

"That's all well and good," Turner said. "But I need proof you're getting minimum wage."

Suddenly the door swung open. A wreath sailed through the air, landing at Turner's feet. "There's your proof," Tammy's husband yelled. "She gets next to nothing for making these stupid things." The door slammed shut.

"Maybe this is a bad time," Allie said.

"No!" Tammy said, red-faced. "My husband's wrong. Without Pop, my kids might go hungry. And come Christmas," she said carefully, glancing at her daughter, "Santa Claus might never make it to this farm."

"All I want to know is how much he pays you an hour. And please," Turner said wearily, "don't tell me it depends."

"Turner, you just don't get it," Allie insisted. "She's telling you what you've heard all day."

"I know," Turner said. "And what I'm hearing is they don't get minimum wage."

"Honey, Daddy needs a hug," Tammy said, pushing the child gently toward the door. She walked down the porch steps and faced Turner.

"Mister, what you're saying doesn't make any sense," she said. "Sure, I might be able to make a wreath in twenty minutes, but I can't time it. My daughter wants me to fix her dolly, I stop. My neighbor comes by for coffee, I stop. You come, I stop. It can take all day to finish one."

"Exactly," Turner said.

"Who's the government to tell me that I can't work in my own home, on my own time, at my own speed?" Tammy shot back. "Pop pays me, but I'm my own boss."

"Not the way the law sees it," he said.

"Then maybe the law's wrong," Allie chimed in.

"Right," Tammy said. "I couldn't do any of this if I punched a clock in town. I'd need a car and a babysitter. Subtract that from minimum wage, and tell me, what's left?"

Turner closed his notebook and turned to Allie. "I've got everything I need," he said.

"This isn't going to hurt Pop, is it?" Tammy said anxiously.

"Don't worry," Allie said. "I'd never let that happen."

In a nearby forest, a pickup bumped along an unpaved road cut through thick stands of pine and holly trees. Around a bend, the surface changed suddenly to a ribbon of asphalt winding in a figure-eight pattern. It was the beginning of a neighborhood. Only the houses were missing.

"This is Holly Estates Phase One," developer Hank Pritchard said.

"And Phase Two?" Pop Henderson said. "That's what my land is for, isn't it?"

Pritchard stopped the truck. "This hasn't been made public yet," he said confidentially. "But DuMar Plastics is planning to locate a new factory just outside Wilford. Engineers, chemists—they're going to want nice houses here in the country."

"Do you know how long it takes to grow the holly trees you're cutting down?" Pop asked.

"A long time," Pritchard acknowledged. "That's what the future's for."

Pop glanced at a wooden sign by the roadside—HOLLY ESTATES: LIVING AT ITS FINEST—and shook his head. "I'm glad I won't be around to see it."

Pritchard put the truck in gear. "You're doing the right thing," he said. "That grandson of yours, he's going to want to go to college. You can't pay for that with holly wreaths." Pritchard stuck out his hand. "You watch, he'll thank you for this."

"Not anytime soon he won't, so let's keep this between us for now," Pop said. He hesitated and then shook Pritchard's hand.

CHAPTER 17

Making Amends

Jeff walked into Swiggett's General Store, pulling a red wagon loaded with canned goods and other items he'd shoplifted.

At the cash register, Mabel looked up from *Modern Romance* and chuckled. "Fred," she called. "You're going to want to come out here."

"What am I supposed to do with this stuff?" Fred said peevishly, looming over the boy. He examined a can of beans. "Nobody's going to want to buy this, banged up the way it is."

Jeff hung his head. "I'm sorry, Mr. Fred."

"Now, Fred," said Mabel. "What about that day-old shelf you were thinking of starting, like the one at the Acme in Wilford?"

"I did, didn't I?" Fred said, smoothing his hair. "Mabel, you know the boy's building a bomb shelter?"

"Not building," Jeff corrected him. "Just stocking the root cellar, you know, in case of nuclear attack."

"Well, that's a smart idea," Fred said, patting Jeff's head awkwardly, adding, "son."

Jeff shrugged, flushing with discomfort. He wondered if Fred would expect to be called "Dad" now that it was official he was marrying his mother.

"Your mom says you're willing to work off the damage," Fred said, hands on his hips, gazing around. "So what are we going to do with you?"

"Floor could use sweeping," Mabel said.

"That's a good start. When you're done, you can wash the windows. I'm going out for a while. Mabel, get the boy what he needs."

"Don't let him bother you none," Mabel told Jeff. "Fred means well, but sometimes he's full of hot air. Let's find that broom." She stopped at the soda cooler. "Sweeping's going to raise a lot of dust. We better get you a pop first."

Allie and John Turner rattled along Route 9 in Pop's pickup, headed back to town under the gunmetal November sky. "Country folks don't have many choices, and you want to take away one of the only ways they can survive," Allie said.

"I don't make the labor laws," Turner said.

"Maybe they need changing. In the city, dogs are kept on a leash. Out here they run free. If they have different laws for dogs, shouldn't there be different ones for people?"

"That's easy to say," Turner countered. "Fact is, some creatures need leashing no matter where they are."

Rounding a bend in the road, Allie downshifted and slowed. "What makes you so sure that people like Pop are always trying to break the rules?"

"Experience."

"Prejudice, I'd say."

"I've got my reasons."

"What? You didn't get a raise once?"

Turner looked out the window. "I wish it were as simple as that," he said softly.

"Maybe you're just jealous."

Turner didn't answer. He pulled out his wallet, removed a yellowed newspaper clipping, and held it up for her to see.

Allie winced at the grainy image of four burly men pummeling a man whose jacket had been yanked over his head.

"That was taken May 26, 1937, outside Henry Ford's River Rouge plant in Dearborn, Michigan. Union organizers had a permit to hand out leaflets. Ford's hired thugs jumped them."

"But why . . . ?" Allie began.

"The man in the middle is my father."

"That's horrible," she said, reaching out and touching his arm.

He pulled it away. "I didn't show you for sympathy—for me or him. You wanted to know why I don't trust bosses. That's why," he said, returning the photo to his wallet. "Not paying a decent wage may not be as bad as beating someone to a pulp, but it's not right. And it keeps people down."

"I'm sorry about your father," Allie said. "But Pop's not like that."

"You do what you have to," Allie said, standing on the platform outside Pop's office with Turner. "But first I want you to know the kind of boss Pop is." She removed the padlock and led him into the storeroom.

Turner smelled the dying wreaths before he saw the piles.

"What is this?" Turner asked.

"Tammy's wreaths," Allie said. "And the wreaths of all the other folks you've met here in Tennyson. Nobody wants them, so Pop hides them in here, and pays for them out of his own pocket."

"Why doesn't he fold?"

"Because people depend on him. I don't know how it is in the city, but here we look out for each other."

"They'd understand," Turner said. "Times change."

"But he can't," Allie said.

Without thinking, Turner reached out to comfort her, then caught himself, and dropped his arm by his side.

CHAPTER 18

A Hot Tip

John Turner drove past Tennyson's shorn cornfields in a state he had never found himself before: on the side of an owner.

He stopped at the Wilford Diner for coffee, hoping to clear his mind for the long drive ahead.

"Sit anywhere you like, hon," the waitress said.

Turner took a booth adjoining one occupied by two men, the only other customers.

"Here's to Holly Estates, Phase Two," one said, toasting with his mug.

"Don't pop the champagne yet, Fred," his companion replied. "Not until Henderson signs on the dotted line. I never thought he'd sell."

"You can thank me for that, Hank. If I hadn't gotten the Labor Department to pay Pop a visit, you'd still be waiting."

Turner shifted in his seat to get a clear view. The man talking smoothed back his hair.

"Nice work, Turner," Wage and Hour Division Chief Raymond Metcalf said, later that day, gleefully swiveling in his chair. "Change of scenery did you good."

"I'm not so sure."

"It's open and shut," Metcalf said, slapping Turner's report from Tennyson.

"It's not that simple," Turner said.

Metcalf's smile vanished. He opened the folder. "Are these figures accurate?"

"Yes, but . . ."

"No buts. These workers aren't paid minimum wage."

"I know," Turner said. "You see, it depends—"

"Depends? You going soft on me?"

"Course not. But things are different down there."

"The law applies to everyone," Metcalf interrupted. "Henderson's breaking the law."

"A law made for city rats," Turner said bitterly.

"And I suppose Henderson's Santa Claus," Metcalf said, resting his elbows on the desk. "It's been real quiet here while you were away. No calls from the mayor or the chamber of commerce. No one breathing down my neck about my hotshot investigator. I like that."

"I'm just saying we could be making a big mistake," Turner said.

"The only mistake I'm making is wasting any more time on this with you. You made your case. Now shut him down."

Metcalf raised his hand to cut off any more debate. "That's an order, Turner. Don't come back until it's done."

The man Turner wanted to see occupied his usual counter seat in the Capitol Diner, engrossed in a paperback. Turner slid onto the adjoining stool. "A little light reading?" he asked his buddy—Peter Doyle of the *Chronicle*.

"Ah, the elusive Mr. Turner reappears," Doyle said, looking up from his book. "Mark Twain is a master storyteller. I'm hoping his talent may rub off."

"I've got a story that'll test your talent," Turner said. "A real tearjerker."

"Let me venture a guess," Doyle said sarcastically, blocking out a headline in the air with his hands. "Downtrodden Immigrants Oppressed by Heartless Sweatshop Owner. John Turner Saves the Day."

"Not even close," Turner said. "I'm talking about a real scoop." Leaning close, he said in a conspiratorial whisper, "Who's the Grinch who stole Christmas?"

Intrigued, Doyle rubbed his chin meditatively. "In this city," he said, "the possibilities are endless."

"How about the U.S. Labor Department?" Turner said.

Doyle closed his book, his eyes wide. "I'm all ears."

Broom in hand, Jeff waited outside Fred's office. Working at Swiggett's General Store wasn't so bad, he decided. Miss Mabel always treated him to a soda and even promised to teach him how to run the register.

Fred was a different story, though, and Jeff already worried about life after the wedding. "There's my way to do something and there's the wrong way" seemed to be his soon-to-be stepfather's favorite expression.

Like sweeping the office stairs. The first time Jeff did it he raised a dust cloud that brought Fred storming from his office in a coughing rage. This time Jeff crept up the stairs on tiptoe, planning to brush each step with slow care. In the stillness, he heard Fred dialing the phone.

"It's been a week since I called you Labor Department fellas to tell you about the problem down here in Tennyson," Fred said, sounding aggrieved. "Now I know your man was nosing around, but Henderson's still in business." He paused. "That a fact?" he continued, pleased now. "I'm mighty glad to hear that. No, my pleasure. Like I said, I care about working folks."

Jeff froze on the steps for a moment, and then began furiously sweeping his way down the steps. By the time Fred charged out, choking on the dust, the boy was gone.

CHAPTER 19

Shutdown

The front door of Swiggett's General Store banged open and Allie stormed in. "Where is he, Mabel?" she demanded. At the back of the store, a light flashed off behind the office one-way mirror. Allie pointed her finger at it. "Fred," she called up angrily. "I want to talk to you." The light came back on.

Fred waited at the top of the stairs, arms outstretched, a nervous smile on his face. Allie asked, "Why, Fred?"

"Why what, darlin'?" he said, backing into the office.

"You know, Fred," she said. "You called the Labor Department on Pop."

Squirming, Fred said, "Where'd you get a foolish notion like that?"

"Jeff heard you, so don't give me any sweet talk. I want to know why."

Fred's eyes shifted as he weighed the benefits of telling the truth. He clasped her hands and launched into a desperate pitch.

"Be rational, Allie," he said. "Time's passed Pop by. Even here in Tennyson, everybody wants plastic wreaths. Pop needed somebody to give him a push."

Allie jerked her hands away and stared at him.

"I don't know what I could have been thinking, that you would be a good father to Jeff."

"Now wait a minute, Allie. The problem is that boy's dishonest."

"Misguided, yes. But that boy acted out of love. He deserves better than you. So do I."

Allie twisted off her engagement ring and dropped it on the desk.

"Allie, come on. What the heck do you think you're doing?"

"Giving you a push," Allie said.

"Allie. Come back here. Right now. Allie." Fred shouted after her. "I did it for the boy. And you. And Pop. For all of us." Through the window, he watched Allie walk down the aisle and out of his life.

Early the next morning, Pop, Allie, and Jeff stood on the platform outside the Holly Wreath Man's office, watching in silence as a freight train slowly rumbled by.

"I remember when it used to stop," Pop said.

"The Holly Wreath Express," Allie said wistfully, linking her arm with his. "Remember when Bobby and I took it up to New York to deliver the Radio City wreath?"

A gray sedan pulled up alongside their pickup. John Turner, grim-faced, got out and limped up the steps.

"Jeff, go sit in the truck," Allie said.

"What is it, Mom? Who is that guy?"

"Mr. Turner. From the Labor Department. Pop and I have business with him. Wait in the truck."

"No way, Mom."

"Let the boy hear it, Allie," Pop said.

Turner held up a piece of paper. "I want you to know this isn't my idea," he told Allie. "I couldn't convince my boss that city rules don't apply out here."

"Bit late for a change of heart, isn't it?" Allie said, skeptically.

"Allie, he's only doing his job," Pop said.

"Pop, don't be so darn reasonable. They've got no right."

"It's been over for a long time," Pop said. "I just didn't want to admit it."

Turner looked over at Jeff and shook his head sadly. "I know what I'm doing to you and all the people around here. It's like shutting Santa down on Christmas Eve." His voice broke. "I've got no choice. I'm sorry."

"It's okay, Turner. Just finish it," Pop said. Jeff walked over and took his grandfather's hand.

"Mr. Henderson," Turner said, struggling to keep his composure. "This is a cease-and-desist order. It bars you from further operations until you can establish that you're in compliance with the minimum wage provisions of the Fair Labor Standards Act."

Turner walked up to the office door and posted the order. "This is wrong," he said.

"I'm sorry, Pop," Allie said.

"It's nobody's fault," Pop said, taking her hand. "It's progress." In the distance, the freight train whistle sounded. "And we got in the way."

Jeff walked to the platform's edge, hands in his pockets, scuffing his sneakers on the concrete.

"Jeff, what is it?" Allie asked.

"Nothing," he shrugged.

"Jeffrey?"

"I guess we won't be going to Radio City this year, huh?"

Allie looked at Pop. "They haven't canceled, Pop."

Jeff brightened. "We could make it on our own, couldn't we?" He looked anxiously from Pop to Turner.

Turner smiled at Jeff. "No law against that," he said.

"Sure," Pop said. "Why not go out with a bang?"

"We'll make the biggest, prettiest wreath anybody's ever seen, Pop," Jeff cried. "We'll show 'em."

CHAPTER 20

Pop's Gift

Jeff hoisted the burlap sack bulging with greenery over his shoulder. On any other November day, he'd rather be climbing trees, but the holly branches in the bag were his ticket to Radio City Music Hall.

Beyond the tree line, something moved. Jeff stepped behind a loblolly pine and peered around it.

A man bundled against the cold crouched behind a tripod, peering through a surveyor's transit. Nearby, another man held a tall measuring stick. Jeff dropped the bag and took off through the woods.

He was out of breath when he reached the house.

"Pop! Mom! Come quick."

"What's wrong?" Allie said in alarm. Pop rose from his armchair, the newspaper spilling to his feet.

"Surveyors!" Jeff said, catching his breath. "On our land."

Pop sank back down.

"Pop, what have you done?" Allie demanded. Pop didn't answer. "Pop, you didn't sell to Hank Pritchard."

"Pop would never sell. Tell her," Jeff pleaded. "As long as we have land we can grow things, we aren't poor. All those things you said, Pop."

"They're measuring for roads and houses," Pop said. "For Holly Estates, Phase Two."

"Pop, why didn't you say anything?" Allie said.

Pop got to his feet and walked to the fireplace. A photograph of a young marine rested on the mantle. He picked it up and passed his hand over the frame.

"Before Bobby left for Korea, we walked in the woods," he said, his back to them. "He was worried about you, Allie, and you too, Jeff, even though you weren't born for a couple of months yet. I promised him I'd always take care of you two." He set the picture down and turned to them.

"I haven't been doing a very good job lately. You and your mom have tried to help, but it's my responsibility. I knew if I sold the land we could finish out the season, Allie. And we'd have enough, Jeff, to put you through college someday. Your dad would want that." Defeated, he dropped into his chair. "For once, I thought I could be like that *Millionaire* show fella."

"But Pop," Allie said, kneeling in front of him. "Why should you have to carry the load?"

"Why not?" he said. "Who should?"

"You're wrong. My dad wouldn't want you to sell," Jeff cried, and ran out of the house.

A pebbled glass door stenciled RAYMOND METCALF, CHIEF, WAGE AND HOUR DIVISION, swung open. "Turner!" Metcalf screamed. He clutched the *Chronicle*, a vein bulging on his forehead. "Get in here!"

Metcalf threw the newspaper on the desk. LABOR DEPARTMENT NIXES COUNTRY CHRISTMAS. He jabbed the headline.

"What's this?" He snatched up the newspaper, scanned the story, and read aloud. "'Some observers likened Wage and Hour Division chief Metcalf to the Grinch who stole Christmas.'" He tossed the paper down. "I look like an idiot."

"I guess they thought it was news," Turner said innocently.

"And who do you suppose they got it from?" Metcalf demanded. "Everybody knows that hack Doyle is your press agent."

"Funny, you always liked his stories before, when we were shutting down sweatshops," Turner said.

"That's different."

"That's what I was trying to tell you," Turner said. "I guess I'm not the only one who sees it that way."

"I don't know what you're trying to accomplish with this stunt. The Holly Wreath Man is shut down. And he's staying that way. You're too late."

Turner nodded. "Maybe," he said. He looked down at the paper. "Maybe not." He pulled out his wallet, removed his badge, and laid it on Metcalf's desk.

"I quit."

"What?" The intercom on Metcalf's desk buzzed. "Chief, it's the Associated Press. It's about the Holly Wreath Man."

"No comment," Metcalf snarled.

Peter Doyle of the *Chronicle* eased into the booth at the Capitol Diner where Turner waited. "This took an inordinate amount of research," Doyle said, pushing a manila envelope across the table.

"If that means 'a lot of digging,' the coffee's on me," Turner said. "How'd you make out?"

"Everything you need's here."

"So, how'd you do it?"

Doyle flashed a sly smile. "I consulted with an expert: Danny Horton's lawyer. I figured if he can keep a crook in business, he can help an honest man get back in." Doyle stirred his coffee. "He was glad to help. Horton's shutting down, moving south. Any jobs for seamstresses in Tennyson?"

"Not that I know of," Turner said. "Doyle, I owe you."

"Anything to help an honest man. Besides, Turner, you inspired me," Doyle said. "I gave my two weeks' notice. It's time I wrote that great American novel. How does *The Holly Wreath Man* strike you as a title?"

CHAPTER 21

Turner's Gift

To stay awake on the long drive to Tennyson, Turner switched on the car radio. The staccato delivery of radio commentator Paul Harvey filled the air.

"Page . . . two." the familiar voice intoned. "Having trouble buying Christmas wreaths for the front door? Not those plastic ones, but the real McCoy, fresh holly from the forest? Thank the U.S. Labor Department, the Scrooge in this Christmas Carol."

Turner laughed, and hoped Metcalf was listening.

"In their bureaucratic wisdom," Harvey continued, "the Feds settled a wage dispute by shutting down Eben Henderson, the Holly Wreath Man, of tiny Tennyson. No merry Christmas for wreath-making farm families denied their only source of income during the cold winter. I know whose stocking I'd like to put a lump of coal in."

❖

Allie opened the kitchen door and set two grocery bags on the table.

"Jeff," she called. "I need help putting the food away."

"Aw, Mom," he begged from the living room. "I'm reading."

Pop lowered his newspaper and shot Jeff a warning glance.

"I'm coming," Jeff said, reluctantly.

The telephone rang. "I'll get it," Pop called. "Dang phone. Ringing off the hook," he muttered.

"Hello," Pop said into the receiver. "Speaking. You're calling from where? How many?" Out of habit, he began taking down the order, then crossed out the message. "I wish I could help," he told the caller, "but I'm not in business anymore. Happy holidays to you, too."

In the kitchen, Allie handed Jeff two cans of beans. He opened the cabinet door. "Not there," she said. "They go downstairs, in the shelter."

"Really?"

"Yep," she said, handing him a bag.

"And there's sugar and creamed corn and coffee in here."

"But I thought—" Jeff said, confused. "What about the stealing?"

"That was wrong. Nothing changes that." She brushed back his cowlick. "But it's important to feel safe. We paid for these, so we can put them where we want."

"Gee, thanks, Mom," Jeff said, hugging her. "You're swell."

"You're a good boy, Jeff. You care about your family. That's what matters most." She kissed him. "Now, what else do you need in a shelter?"

"I've got a list up in my room. I'll get it." Jeff started to run out, then stopped. "I'll finish putting the food away first."

"I've got it." She smiled. "Get your list."

"Okay, but I can already tell you," he said, breathless with excitement. "We need crackers, cookies, powdered milk." He dashed upstairs, calling out a litany of supplies. "Tuna fish, peanut butter, fruit juice, baked beans . . ."

The phone rang again. "Hello," Pop said. "You want how many?"

The phone in Pop's office started ringing early the next morning. "Hold your horses," Pop said, climbing the platform stairs with Jeff and Allie.

"I told you, Mom," Jeff said. "Everybody wants Christmas from the forest."

"I know. Isn't it wonderful, Pop?" Allie said.

"No, it's not. I'm shut down. Just like it says here," Pop said, waving at the cease-and-desist order on the door. "I can't put anybody to work, remember?"

"Actually, Mr. Henderson, that's not true."

John Turner emerged from the shadows at the end of the platform, looking like a man who had driven all night.

"What are you doing here?" Allie bristled. "Haven't you caused enough trouble?"

"Yes, ma'am, I have," Turner said. "But I'd like to try to set it right."

"How?" she said.

He held up a manila envelope. "A cooperative."

"A what?" Jeff said.

"It's an association, Jeff," Turner explained. "People come together to make things and sell them. They share the work and the profits."

They all looked at Pop. In the distance, a freight train whistle blew. Pop tore the order off the door. "It sounds like a fine way to do business. Now let me get that phone."

"Why are you doing this?" Allie said.

"I don't know," Turner said. "I guess I'm tired of chasing city rats."

"You want a hundred wreaths?" Pop's voice boomed. "No, no problem. The Holly Wreath Cooperative can handle it."

"What about your job?" Allie said.

"I'm looking for a new one," Turner said.

"Ever make a wreath?"

Turner smiled and shook his head.

Allie put her arm around her son. "Jeff, I think we need to teach Mr. Turner how to make a holly wreath."

CHAPTER 22

Tennyson's Gift

Two days before the giant Radio City wreath was due in New York, the newest member of the Holly Wreath Cooperative vanished. "Pop, have you seen Turner?" Allie asked.

"Haven't laid eyes on him," Pop said. He lifted the office phone off the hook and shut the receiver in his desk drawer. "Only way I can get any peace," he said.

Ever since the *Chronicle* story went national, the phone hadn't stopped ringing. Pop's wreath makers struggled to keep up as out-of-towners descended on Tennyson to buy wreaths for their homes and stores called in rush orders. Jeff and Turner emptied the storeroom of Pop's dying discards and restocked it with fresh ones.

Olivia Coffin, Pop's oldest supplier, took over as cashier, finishing wreaths in between sales. Pop hummed Christmas carols and chewed antacid, never busier—or happier.

"Weren't the two of you here late last night?"

Allie blushed. "Pop, we were making wreaths."

"Of course you were," Pop said, straight-faced. "Turner's probably getting some shut-eye. You could use some, too."

"Look who's talking. Pop, when's the last time you got some rest?"

"No time. I don't see how we're going to make it," he fretted. "All these orders keep pouring in, and the Radio City wreath is still not done. Where's Jeff?"

"Here, Pop," Jeff said, walking in the door, laden with wreaths.

"Come on. We've got some business to take care of." Pop opened the desk drawer and handed Allie the phone. "It's all yours."

"Jeff," Allie said, "have you seen Turner?"

"No, Mom. His car's not here."

Pop turned off Route 9 onto a dirt road—the family's shortcut to their holly woods. A new sign greeted them: "Holly Estates, Phase Two."

"Pop," Jeff said, "where are we going?"

"To cut holly for the Radio City wreath. There's nowhere near enough back in the storeroom."

"But Pop, wouldn't that be stealing from Mr. Pritchard?"

"Yes, it would be," he said, ruefully, stopping the truck. "If we didn't own the land."

"But I thought—"

"You were right, Jeff. Your dad wouldn't sell because he'd want you to have this," Pop said. "And you're going to want your kids to have it, too. I told Pritchard the deal was off. So hop out and pull up that sign."

By noon, Allie had given up on Turner. She passed Olivia a red bow.

"Maybe the country's boring for a man who's spent his life in the city," she said.

"Don't give up on him yet," Olivia said, patting Allie's hand.

The office door banged open. "Mom, Turner's back. You've gotta see this!"

"Told you," Olivia said.

Allie hurried out to the platform. John Turner stood by the Tennyson school bus, helping a line of chattering women down the steps.

"Danny Horton's seamstresses needed work," he said. "Think you can teach them how to make a wreath, Allie?"

For the first time that day, Allie smiled. "If I can teach you, Turner, I can teach anyone," she said. "Come on in, ladies. We've got plenty to do."

They worked nonstop for hours. The seamstresses took quickly to wreath making. Outside on the platform, under Pop's watchful eye, Jeff and Turner hammered an oversized frame for the Radio City wreath.

Night fell, casting the platform in shadow. "We're not going to make it," Pop worried. "We need to leave for New York, but I can't see a thing out here."

"Can't quit now, Pop. You're putting Tennyson on the map," Fred Swiggett called, climbing the platform steps, carrying a cardboard box. Mabel, lugging two thermoses, followed. "We've got coffee, sandwiches, and doughnuts."

"Day-old," Mabel whispered to Jeff.

"I brought reinforcements, too," Fred said. Three trucks pulled up, their lights illuminating the platform. "The boys at the store heard you needed help. They've rounded up all the old-timers." More cars and pickups converged, bathing the scene in bright light.

"There you go, Pop," Turner said, "all the light you need."

Their headlights turned night into day. Country folk and city seamstresses worked side by side in the cold, warmed by hot coffee and laughter. The Radio City wreath slowly took shape as they wrapped the frame with thick boughs of prickly emerald leaves and bright clusters of red berries. Olivia and Allie guided the seamstresses as they sewed ornaments—silver bells, gold balls, and glittery pinecones. As dawn broke, they attached the crowning jewel: an immense red velvet ribbon.

"It's a beauty, Pop," Jeff said.

Pop opened his mouth. No words came out.

"Pop!" Allie cried.

Turner caught Pop just as his legs buckled.

CHAPTER 23

Allie's Choice

Y ou stubborn old mule," said Dr. Quillen, a coat draped over his pajamas, as he listened to Pop's chest through a stethoscope. "What did I tell you about taking it easy?"

Pop squirmed in his desk chair. "Taking it easy is for loafers like you," he snapped.

"I'm sorry, doctor," Allie said remorsefully. "It's all my fault. I should have made him go home."

"Nonsense, I'm not an invalid," Pop said, struggling to his feet. "Now stand aside, sawbones. I've got a wreath to deliver."

"You're not going anywhere except to bed," Dr. Quillen said, gently pushing Pop back down. "At home or in the hospital. Your choice."

"I've got to get to New York City," he insisted. "Allie and Jeff can't make the drive on their own."

Fred Swiggett stepped forward. "I'll take them, Pop." He smoothed back his hair and looked over at Allie. "It's the least I can do."

Allie hesitated. "That's kind of you, Fred, but—"

"Maybe Mr. Turner could drive," Jeff chimed in, looking hopefully at his mother.

Pop looked up at Turner. "You used to work in New York City, didn't you?" he said.

Turner nodded, glancing at Allie. "I'd be glad to help," he said. "But if you'd rather—"

"That settles it then," Olivia Coffin announced. "Let's get that wreath in the truck, get you three on the road, and you," she said firmly to Pop, "into bed."

Jeff slept most of the drive to New York City, giving Turner and Allie a chance to talk. She told him about Bobby, her high school sweetheart who went off to Korea and came home in a flag-draped casket.

"He was a lot like Pop," she said. "Headstrong and good-hearted." She glanced down at her son, sleeping between them. "He's a lot like his father."

Turner described his adventures as a Labor Department investigator, soft-pedaling the danger and loneliness, and told her about the woman he nearly married until she decided his work was too much competition.

They discovered they shared a favorite movie, *It's a Wonderful Life,* both admired President Kennedy and, for the life of them, couldn't understand the appeal of Elvis Presley. Talking like old friends, they barely noticed the miles and hours slipping by. At dusk, Turner steered the pickup onto Manhattan's Avenue of the Americas.

"Wake up, Jeff," Allie said. "We're here."

"Already?" Jeff said, rubbing his eyes and stretching. Through the windshield, he saw Radio City Music Hall for the first time and gasped. The marquee, a shimmering red-and-blue neon sign that seemed to go on forever, advertised his dream, "Christmas Spectacular Starring the Rockettes."

Jeff, Allie, and Turner watched from the sidewalk as workers astride tall ladders hoisted Tennyson's holly wreath into the air. The three of them held their breath until the wreath was firmly secured to the blue neon bands running parallel along the bottom of the marquee.

"I wish Pop could see it," Jeff said.

Allie hugged him. "You can tell him all about it when we get home."

As a favor to Pop, the stage manager put them in the front row for the Rockettes' ninety-minute show. The lights dimmed, Christmas music from the giant Wurlitzer organ filled the cavernous theater, the curtain parted, and there they were: a chorus line of thirty-six high-kicking goddesses in green velvet trimmed in white fur.

Jeff sat on the edge of his seat, gaping as the Rockettes transformed themselves over and over, into candy canes, wooden soldiers, dancing dolls. He glanced sideways and smiled. His mother and Turner were holding hands and—he couldn't believe it—were sound asleep in their seats. It must be a sign of old age, he decided. How could anyone doze off when the Rockettes were on stage?

The organ music swelled. A menagerie of camels, llamas, horses, and sheep filled the stage for the "Living Nativity" number. Jeff's eyelids drooped. He blinked furiously, shook his head, trying to fight an over-whelming urge to close his eyes.

Unable to resist, Jeff fell asleep.

But he could still see the Rockettes, dancing before him.

CHAPTER 24

A Dream Come True

Onstage at Radio City Music Hall, a Rockette dressed as a red-sequined Santa's Helper leaned over and whispered to a boy sleeping in the front row.

"The show's over," the dancer said. "It's time to go home."

She stepped back into the chorus line.

"Goodbye, Jeff." The Rockettes waved in unison. "They're waiting for you."

"Jeff. Jeff."

"Daddy?"

Jeff's eyes fluttered open. His mother, silver-haired, stood at his bedside.

"Mom?" he said. Next to her, a boy and girl stared anxiously down at him.

Jeff's confusion turned to joy.

"Will! Katie!"

"Daddy," they cried, throwing themselves at him.

At the foot of the bed stood an older man with a familiar lined face, the stranger who came to town one Thanksgiving and ended up marrying his mother.

"Hey, Turner," Jeff said.

"Hey there, buddy," Turner said, coming over and clasping his hand. "Long time no see."

"You'd be surprised," Jeff said.

It all came back to him: The kids running away, getting snowed in on the farm, falling on the cellar stairs, and the longest, and best, night's sleep he'd had in years.

"You scared us, Daddy," Katie said, crossing her arms against her chest.

"We came in this morning," Will said, "and you wouldn't wake up."

"It's probably a mild concussion from that fall," his mother said. "Doc Quillen's coming by to check on you."

Jeff touched the lump on his head and winced. "That old coot?" Jeff said. "He can't still be around."

"Goodness no," Allie laughed. "His granddaughter."

"I called Mom," Will said.

For the first time he noticed the younger woman in the doorway.

"Rachel?"

"I borrowed my dad's four-wheel drive," she explained, coming in and wrapping her arms around the children. "I got here as fast as I could."

Overcome, Jeff could only whisper, "Thank you."

Outside the bedroom window, the sky shone a brilliant, cloudless blue. All was quiet except for the scraping sound of a snow plow.

"Route 9 should be cleared soon," his mother said. "Turner and Will shoveled the drive. You'll be able to get out now."

Jeff swung his legs over the bed. "I'm starved. Any of those biscuits left, Mom?"

Will and Katie looked at each other guiltily. "We kind of ate them all, Dad," Will said.

Turner and Allie laughed. "I can make more," Allie said. "You get dressed, Jeff. And you two," she told her grandchildren, "come down and help Grandpa and me in the kitchen. We've got pies to make for tomorrow's dinner."

The four of them trooped downstairs, leaving Jeff and Rachel alone.

"Are you really okay?" she said, breaking the awkward silence.

"I'm not sure." Jeff touched the back of his head. "I think so. I had a very weird dream."

"It's a good thing the doctor's coming to see you," Rachel said.

"But what about you? I know you had plans, but . . ."

Downstairs the phone rang. "I'll get it," Will shouted.

"Rachel, is there any way," Jeff said, fumbling, "you could stay and spend the holiday with us?"

"I'm not sure that's a good idea, Jeff," Rachel said.

Will appeared in the doorway. "It's your office, Dad," he said sullenly. "And Grandma says your biscuits are ready."

"Finally!" Cheryl, Jeff's assistant, said. "How are you?"

"Couldn't be better," he said.

"Well, you're in luck. The storm shut down the whole city. They're rescheduling the meeting for the day after Thanksgiving. If you can get back online, I'll e-mail you the info. Send me what you've got and I can put the presentation together."

"Hold it, Cheryl," Jeff said. "I don't have anything to send."

"What? I thought you were okay."

"Oh, I'm more than okay." Will and Rachel stared at him. "It's just that things here in the country don't move as fast. I don't know when the roads will be clear enough for me to get out of here." He winked at Will.

"You know what?" he said into the phone. "Ask Sue if she'll take over the presentation. She deserves a chance to prove herself. Might as well put that MBA of hers to work. We're going to stay here for the holiday." He laughed and said reassuringly, "It's okay, Cheryl, I'm fine, believe me. Happy holiday. See you next week."

"For real, Dad?"

Jeff knew a dream couldn't change everything, but that bump on his head had taught him one thing: Nothing mattered more than his family.

He looked at Rachel. "For real."

CHAPTER 25

The Holly Wreath Man

I'm stuffed," Jeff groaned. He pushed back from the dining room table, littered with the remains of a country-style holiday feast, and smiled at his family.

"You better have room for pie," Rachel said. "We haven't been baking all day for nothing."

"That's right, Daddy," Katie said. "We made apple, cherry, and . . ."

"I made the pumpkin," Will interrupted.

"And I'm sure they're delicious," Jeff said. "But if I don't walk off Grandma's turkey and stuffing first, I'm going to burst."

Turner patted his belly. "Your dad's right." He gazed across the table at Allie.

"What do you say we all take a walk in the woods?"

"Let's show them Pop's favorite tree," Jeff said.

"While we're out there we can cut some fresh holly," Allie said. "Then we can make Christmas wreaths."

"Can we, Mom?" Will asked, looking at Rachel.

"Sure. That's a great idea," said Rachel, "But let's get bundled up," she told the kids. "It's cold outside."

A short while later, the six of them trudged through the woods among stands of pine and holly trees, their branches sagging under thick coats of snow.

In a clearing, Jeff stopped before a lone holly tree, so tall and full and green it seemed to blot out the sky.

"Here it is," he said.

"Wow!" Will said.

"Pop always claimed it was the biggest in the state," Allie said. "It's the one we always used for the Radio City wreath. Remember, Jeff?"

Jeff nodded. "I wish he could be here."

"Me, too," his mother said, putting her arm around his shoulder. "I know he'd like to see his great-grandchildren, and their mother." Allie took Rachel's hand.

"Pop was right about one thing," Jeff said. "It would have been a mistake to sell this land."

"That's for sure," Turner said, clipping off branches. "We could never have kept Pop's nursery business going without it."

"That's what I was hoping to talk to you about this weekend, Jeff," Allie said. "It's getting to be too much for us."

They followed the setting sun home. Jeff carried a burlap sack filled with holly. The kids ran ahead, lobbing snowballs at each other and shrieking with pleasure. "They're really happy out here," Rachel said.

"So Jeff," his mother said with a twinkle in her eye, "what would you do with a million dollars?"

He laughed, remembering the game they used to play when he was a child. He stopped and breathed in the crisp air, tinged with wood smoke. He looked at his children up ahead, and back at his wife.

"Not a thing, Mom," he said. "I've got everything I want."

He paused and looked at Rachel. "On second thought, I don't know. Maybe buy a nursery business."

That evening, Jeff and his family sat rosy-cheeked at the kitchen table, washing down slices of pie with hot cocoa, surrounded by coils of baling wire, ornaments, ribbons, and the shiny holly boughs they'd collected on their walk.

"Show me how, Daddy," Katie said. "I want to make one."

"How about you, Will?"

"Yeah," Will nodded. "They're cool, Dad."

"First, pick out some branches."

"I want one with lots of berries," Katie said.

"Fasten the branches together with wire, twisting it tightly under the leaves," Jeff said, guiding them. "Careful, the leaves are sharp. Shape the connected branches into a circle. Tie the ends together. And you've each got a wreath." Two shiny green circles lay on the table in front of them.

"That's it?" Will said.

"Now you have to decorate it," Jeff said. "How about a red ribbon and some gold bells?" Jeff tied the red velvet strip into a plump bow. He threaded wire through the bow's knot, concealing it, and attached it to the wreath.

"There you go. Christmas from the forest."

"Awesome, Dad!" Will said.

"Now, you two put on the bells," Jeff said.

"I'm going to hang mine on my bike when I get home," Katie said.

That night, after the kids were tucked in bed and Allie and Turner had said goodnight, Jeff and Rachel sat before the living room fire.

"You're pretty good at making wreaths," she said.

"I've had lots of practice. I swear I was making them in my sleep," he said. "There's one more I'm going to make this weekend. A fancy one. For you."

Rachel stared at the flames. She took his hand in hers.

"I'd like that," she said. "On one condition."

"What's that?"

"You come home," she said. "And hang it on our front door."

Once again, Jeff Henderson's life was full. But not too full, because now, it was full of happiness.